BLACK GENEALOGY

The Mineral Point Poetry Series

Tanka & Me
Kaethe Schwehn

My Seaborgium
Alicia Rebecca Myers

Fair Day in an Ancient Town
Greg Allendorf

My Tall Handsome
Emily Corwin

A Wife Is a Hope Chest
Christine Brandel

Black Genealogy
Kiki Petrosino

The Mineral Point Poetry Series 6
Kiki Petrosino, Editor

BLACK GENEALOGY

poems

by Kiki Petrosino

with illustrations by
Lauren Haldeman

Brain Mill Press
Green Bay, Wisconsin

Some of the poems in this collection have appeared previously in the following publications and are reprinted here with permission: *Miracle Monocle:* "1 [You're on a train]"

Hampden-Sydney Poetry Review: "2.2 [We only woke up when you called us]"; "2.4 [You ask why we didn't register as required]"; "2.5 [What is it like, to still have a body]"

The poem "6 [You wake up because]" was interpreted by choreographer Shelby Shenkman and performed at the Louisville Ballet.

Published in the United States by Brain Mill Press.
Print ISBN 978-1-942083-73-3
EPUB ISBN 978-1-942083-76-4
MOBI ISBN 978-1-942083-74-0
PDF ISBN 978-1-942083-75-7

www.brainmillpress.com

The Mineral Point Poetry Series, number 6.
Published by Brain Mill Press, the Mineral Point Poetry Series is edited by Kiki Petrosino. In odd years, the series invites submissions of poetry chapbooks around a theme. In even years, the editor chooses a full collection.

BLACK GENEALOGY

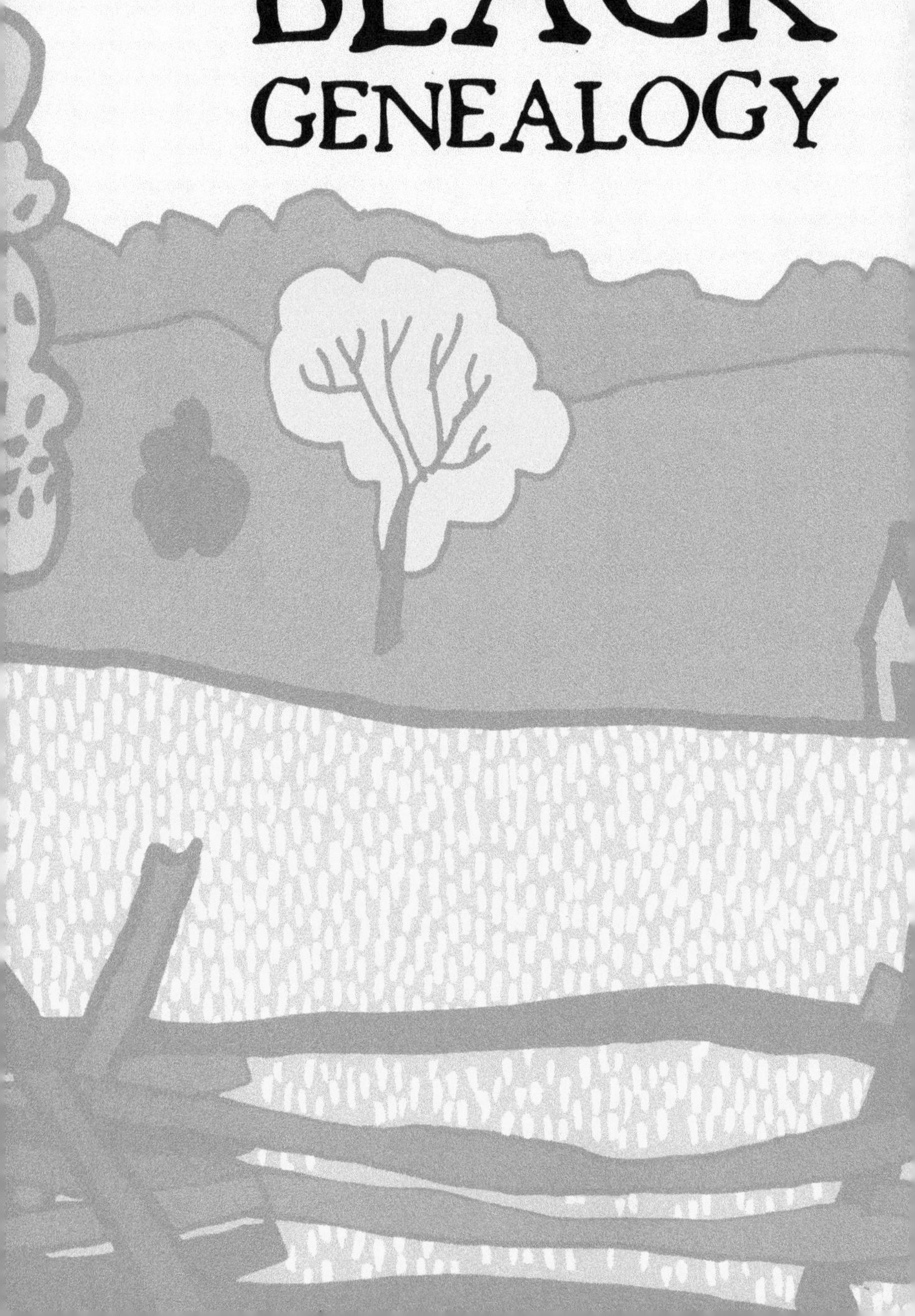

Please, would you tell me
you ask the Cashier
a little timidly
for you're still
not sure it's a good idea
OPEN
to speak to anyone

at the battlefield shoppe
CIVIL WAR
LEE
why that Man is
grinning like that?

He's playing a Confederate General today
says the Cashier
& that's why
You say:
I didn't know Confederate Generals always grinned.
In fact, I didn't know Confederate Generals could grin.
They all can
says the Cashier
& most of 'em do.

ONE

1.

You're on a train & your ancestors are in the Quiet Car. The Quiet Car is locked with a password you can't decrypt. You're a professional password decrypter & your ancestors are professional demolition experts. You're wearing black tactical gear & your ancestors are wearing black tactical gear. You're moving back through the train, slamming doors open, & your ancestors are ahead of you, laying small explosive charges in your path. When your ancestors blow up the Quiet Car, you escape through a window hatch. You climb to the top of the train & your ancestors rappel down the sides. You're rappelling down one side of the train when you glimpse your ancestors above you, again, leaping from car to car. You cling to the train & your ancestors lift right off the roof with the help of multiple jetpacks. And lo, your ancestors are hundreds of slow snake doctors, & lo, your ancestors, intensively spinning. The train enters a tunnel & the train exits a tunnel. You, on the other hand, have been missing for some time.

2.

B is for *bright*. A boy. No birthmarks but his hair (*inclined to straightness*) & his nose (*more like a white man's*). *B*, also, for the bluets you dreamed, crowding the edge of the drive leading up to the old farm you've crossed two states to see. What will you do if you find no parcel in the name of *B*? At the courthouse, in the chamber, at the indicated plat? Only the dumb columns of noughts you scroll in the relic room, white ingot of fear as you look. So sorry you don't already know the yard where chickens pecked & patted under the eye of granddaddy *B*. So sorry you missed him on his way. He must be burning high above your head, a comet, or worse. The story of a comet somebody told. Wrong comet, wrong county. Wrong dates spiraled into the roll book. One roll of microfilm for every year you can't confirm. How to confirm a certain garden gate or palings not marked on any grid? Lucky *B*, spangled *B*. This is not where you begin.

3.

You're really looking for *H*, future mother of *B*. A slave girl born in 1830 to parents unknown. Actually, you think *H* was born a little before that (exact years may not matter). You find a white man in the county who owned a young female some years before the war. You save this result: *Old_Master*. You figure that by 1856, your *H* was 28. Actually, no one recorded her age (her age may not matter). That year, a slave named *H* gave birth to a son. You save this result: *H_Childbirth_1*. Later, another *H*, same owner as the first (now called *H56*) had a son. You start calling her *H59*. Actually, you believe they're the same. Of course, you can't prove that *H56* and *H59* are the same, let alone yours, but exact proof may not matter. You know Old Master owned twelve slaves at most. So what are the chances two of them were called *H*? You still can't find any sign of *B*, which troubles you. Until you discover the birth records for the war period: all missing. So of course, there's nothing for *B* at the courthouse. Nothing at all. You create a new folder called *Nothing* for this lucky find.

4.

They say *B*'s house had so many wings it looked like a sleeping hawk. They say a family of whitefolks built it. Enough verandas for everyone to have a secret view of the place, each railing painted to match the trees, so you felt you were stepping on clear air when you went out there with your mug of morning tea. The whitefolks kept a library of pine seeds in the cellar & gardening books on stands in the hall. But something happened. They got in their wagon & said: *take care of this till we get back.* Which is the only way, they say, a man like *B* could get a house with so many grand porches on every floor. They say, *blacks weren't meant to look down on the world from a height.* Except, *B* did. So you start to think of the land as his book. He wrote what he wished.

5.

Old Master writes the names you seek in his ledgers, or might do. It depends on what Old Master sees, what subtleties he tracks, which gifts. *Abby walked to Oatlands*, he writes in 1864, but you need to read, *H walked*. You need her to come up from the quarter & step through the narrow ring of Old Master's attention, *a light girl with ears bored for rings.* But *H* is prudent. She never wastes her scant yard of brown tecklenburg or breaks her tools in the field like the others. For a whole page, instead of talking about *H*, Old Master counts his glass decanters from France. He orders *every hand to finish harvest* without saying whose hands. You search for *H* until the yellow globes of Old Master's script go dim, gummed like the fallen chinaberry fruit about his house. Well, well. It's a good thing you're a finch now. You were born to gorge.

6.

You wake up because you hear someone singing *little lamb, little lamb*, as if the singer were calling from across a great distance. You know, as you've always known, that you're the *little lamb* in this song, just as you know that no matter how prominent your streak of grey, the singer of this particular song will always sing, *little lamb*, meaning you, quite distinctly. As you climb from the covers, you try to tell the song to *stop that noise, please* but what comes out is *play it again* which you hadn't meant to say, at all. Soon, the song starts up once more, unfolding the long journey of itself, of twisting through pine forests & leaping up hundreds of tall gardens arranged like stairs. The song even describes you, in some time before you remember. You wore a suit of woven water & learned to speak in rippling syllables. You, or someone like you.

7.

You don't love *B*, exactly. You love the wagon of his name, long letters filling up with leaves & peeling bark. You love walking around Old Town, imagining *B*'s voice calling *haw!* to his horses, a sound to strike the chilly cobbles at night. Almost nothing from that time survives but the courthouse, the occasional hat rack in a restaurant, & those cobbles, reddish & packed like reptile scales in the streets. Of course, the cobbles only look special to you because of *B*, unloading his wagon before the post office building, which blurs into a modern gastropub serving small batch bourbon. How quickly your *B*, too, unfolds into other *B*s, each one alive in his own Old Town. If you could reach into every successive *B*, past the springs & bolsters of his mind, you'd pull out infinite thumb-sized replicas of yourself, standing outside the gastropub, your glass of bourbon an unpainted bud repeated time after time.

8.

To locate *B*, you must learn to move in two directions. Find the war & begin to pace the decades forward, then back. Carry on your person the Hotchkiss map of the zone you're searching, plus a handwritten list of relatives' names under the heading *cloud of witnesses*. If you reach your mother in her red raincoat, if you can hear her calling you from the woods, you've gone too far. Start again from the depot. A train will transport you to 1870, the next census after the war, but you won't be permitted to disembark unless *B* appears. To be honest with you, no one in this county has ever disembarked at 1870; witness the platform for that year, covered in wasps. You'll have to start again from the depot & walk until you reach the 1850 slave schedule. Here, you'll first glimpse Old Master on a wooden bench, surrounded by the members of his white & black households in various states of service. We advised you to carry your *cloud of witnesses* precisely for moments like this. Some names will repeat over multiple persons, while others have no names at all. You have only to lay your *cloud of witnesses* over the scene & wait for a match. Any shape you see could be yours.

9.

When they turn *B*'s town into a stop on the Heritage Trail, you luck into a room at the local inn. The concierge stamps your promotional passport, good for a long weekend of shoppes & spa days: *Commonwealth Full Body Facial. Sacajawea's Aromatherapy Journey.* The place is a gem of an Old South *jardin*, comfortably appointed. You try an egg. A plank of pure country ham. You stretch your boots across the live oak floor. Everyone's so cheerful here, above the malaria belt & below the typhoid zone, between States which fought a war that no one names just now. That rushing sound comes from several artesian springs, & you may drink from every one. You may sit in the center of a large shady lawn, on a summer evening, while the proprietor sets dozens of Japanese lanterns on little tables. Your waiter hands you a single oyster fork, the better to pierce through your skull at any time. No one shall say a word.

Where did you say you were staying?
asks the Man Dressed as a Confederate General.
You hadn't said, actually.
I heard you were looking for family the General continues.
Me, too you finally say.
We care a good deal here, about family.
I'd like to learn what happened here.
Oh, you're sure to do that says the General
if only you stay long enough.

You feel this cannot be denied, so you try a question.
What can you tell me about the free people who lived around here?
Oh, the General answers, brushing fluff from his coat. We're all free here. I'm free. You're free.
How do you know I'm free? you ask.
You must be says the General. Or you wouldn't have come here.
You don't think that proves it all; however, you go on: And how do you know that you're free?
To begin with says the General
I belong to certain organizations. Organizations for which you must prove your pedigree. I couldn't wear this uniform without proving it. You grant that?
I suppose so you say.
Well, then.

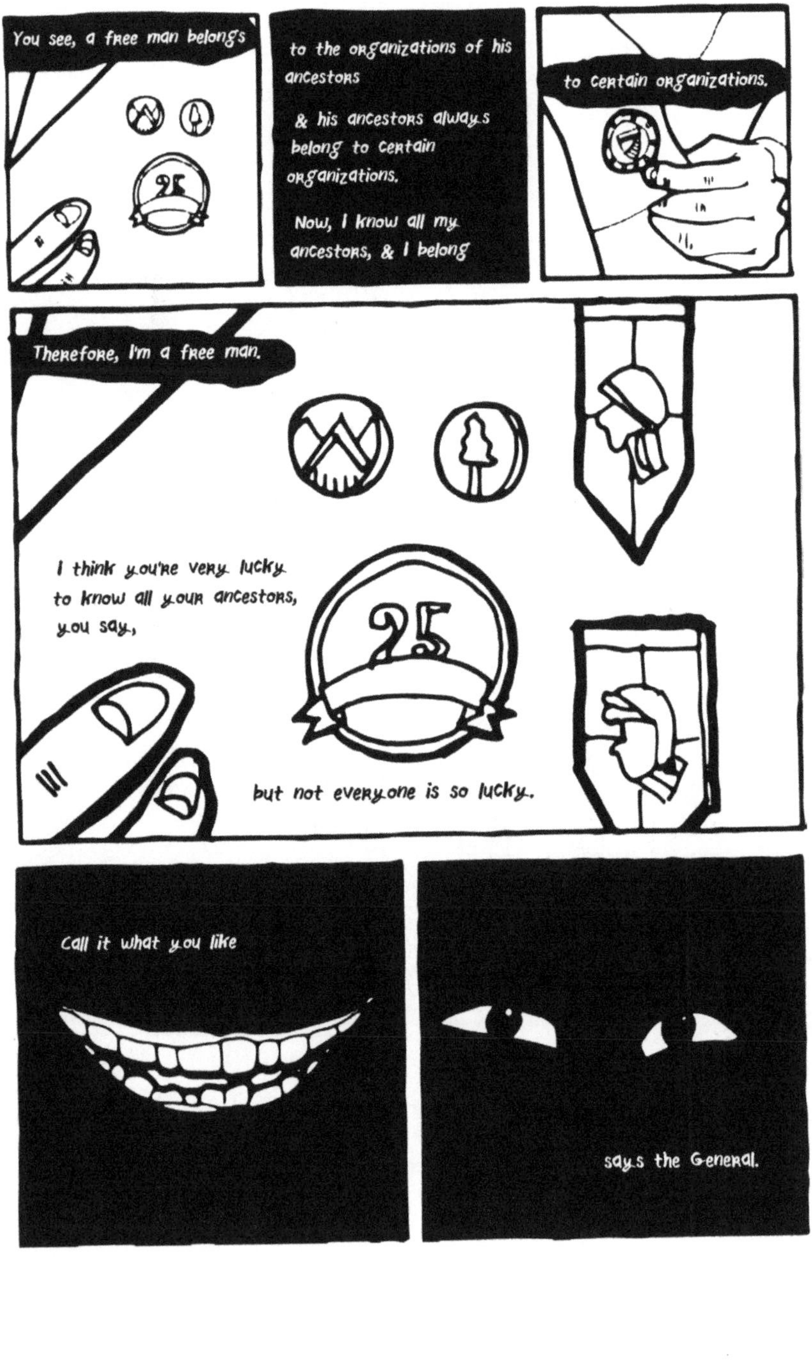
You see, a free man belongs
to the organizations of his ancestors
& his ancestors always belong to certain organizations.
Now, I know all my ancestors, & I belong
to certain organizations.
Therefore, I'm a free man.
25
I think you're very lucky to know all your ancestors, you say,
but not everyone is so lucky.
Call it what you like
says the General.

TWO

1.

You want to know who owned us & where.
But when you type, your searches return no results.
Slavery was grown folks' business, then old folks'.

We saw no reason to hum Old Master's name
to our grandchildren, or point out his overgrown gates
but you want to know who owned us & where

we got free. You keep typing our names into oblongs
of digital white. You plant a unicode tree & climb up
into grown folks' business. You know old folks

don't want you rummaging here, so you pile sweet jam
in your prettiest dish. You light candles & pray:
Tell me who owned you & where

I might find your graves. Little child, we're at rest
in the acres we purchased. Those days of
slavery were old folks' business. The grown folks

buried us deep. Only a few of our names survive.
We left you that much, sudden glints in the grass.
The rest is grown folks' business we say. Yet
you still want to know. Who owned us? Where?

2.

We only woke up when you called us.
When you tracked our graves with your satellites.
No one said our names for a hundred years

but now we stirred. We'd nearly forgotten
that feeling; you sound just like our babies.
We always woke up when they called us

for milk, no matter how late. No matter
how weary. The heat of the quarter, in summer—
For a hundred years, no one said our names.

Then you arrived at the edge of the woods.
Our tombstones are small. The trees have grown close.
When you called us, we woke up

hoping. Did you bring a sharp blade to break up
these weeds? Can't remember which kind is best.
No one has said our names for a hundred years

so we lie here, trying to describe the last color
we saw. If the air between trees were a word: *almost*.
But no one has said our names for a hundred years.
When you call us, we'll wake.

3.

We weren't truly free until
we read the Amendment ourselves
all the way to Lincoln's signature, dark vines

gathering over the page. *A. Lincoln* said we
should go forth, leaving bondage forever
but we weren't truly free until

we signed our own names & read them
back to ourselves. Our names, not our marks
dark vines gathered at *X*. Lincoln's signature

was always so calm, a brown river of stones
worn smooth with patience. We had no time
to catch up. We weren't truly free until

we'd scaled the high turret of *B* or unlatched
the strap where *H* buckles itself. Still, it took years
to reach Lincoln's signature, dark vines

gathering. Our jagged serifs serrated the pages
we signed. We wrote out our wills. You write
poems about Lincoln, dark little vines of *until*.
What do you know about freedom?

4.

You ask why we didn't register as required
why we failed to appear before the Provost Marshal
why we avoided the courthouse, the census, the bank.

You ask where we sheltered while battles seethed
where our mothers gave birth, in which hidden houses
& why we didn't register as required.

While so many of us perished
or raged with Nat in Southampton, how did we manage?
We avoided the courthouse, the census, the bank.

Whatever we had, we held onto. Whatever we knew
we told no one who counted. We kept back
our names. We didn't register as required.

When you search for us now, you find silence.
You may trace us back to a moment. No further.
We avoided the courthouse, the census, the bank

for a reason. To live. That was always our answer.
So we chose inward passages. We kept our own counsel.
We didn't register as required, which disappoints you.
Why do you trust the courthouse, the census, the bank?

5.

What is it like, to still have a body?
Like insects, or velvet—we almost remember.
That's why we sent you the dreams.

Something green. Something moving.
We remember holding the rain in our mouths.
We think: *it's like that, to still have a body.*

Furious burst of blood from the dirt—
Thousands of white seeds, falling—
That's why we sent you. The dreams

keep our wishes walking. We're lonely
without music to play in our hollow.
You still have a body. What is it like?

We almost remember the air
on our tongues: silk of violets, linen of sky.
It's why we sent you the dreams

of walking through drifts of peeling bark—
of mirrors that hang by themselves in dark halls—
You can dream because you still have a body.
Tell us what it's like.

6.

Great storms shook Old Master's house
several times in a week. The land shone, then
incessant, bright & awful—we thought

the spirits of our dead mothers had finally
crossed the sea. Old Master's babies died
as great storms shook his house. Dishes

broke. Drawers opened. We watched
our dead mothers pull out baby clothes—
incessant, bright & awful, we thought

as they shredded with their wet hands
the lace bibs Old Master's wife had stitched
while great storms shook the house.

Then Old Master's wife ordered us
to rip the stays from her gowns. She walked
incessant, bright & awful. We thought

she'd walk into the earth. We had to feed
her babies with our milk before they died
incessant, bright & awful. The land shone
on the great house. Our dead swarmed.

7.

Old Master called us his "outlying Negroes."
We managed his bakehouse. His shops & his fields.
We knew how to make jubilee

after we cleared Old Master's meadows. After we
twisted the ropes of tobacco he sold to the English.
We were Old Master's "outlying Negroes."

When preachers & exhorters came, we stood
in the weaving house with Old Master & listened.
We already knew how to make jubilee. In the woods

we held our own meetings. Now we named
our sons: Moses, Aaron. Old Master approved.
We were his outlying Negroes

& we made jubilee. In the bakehouse, the schoolroom.
In shops & in fields. We got baptized right next
to Old Master. We made jubilee with him

large in his silks. We shared the same sabbath.
We worshipped together. You wonder how that
could be true, but it is. Business & jubilee were the same
back there, in the outlying lands.

8.

Flushed with notions of freedom
you follow the old wood road to its end.
B's acreage opens up behind fence posts

a spill of storybook umber. Even the light
between birches feels thicker now
flushed with notions of freedom.

For a moment, you wonder if the land
will dissolve before you can rush forward.
Then you're over the fence, on *B*'s acreage

where deer blinds hang like aerial masks.
You gather your private handful of acorns,
flushed with emotion. Freedom is old here

despite the long aisles of trail cameras
looking down from their greying trunks.
What can harm you on *B*'s acreage? Open

your stride to cover more ground. *Any
descendant may access a grave*, says the law
you printed before climbing the fence.
You're free, for now. Enjoy the rush.

After a minute or two you walk on in the direction in which your ancestors were said to live.

You're not much surprised
by the General's disappearance
as you're getting used
to such things happening.
But while you're passing
by the place
where the General had been
he suddenly appears again.

Bythe bye, what became of your family? I'd nearly forgotten to ask.
You quietly say: They survived. But they didn't stay here after the war.
I thought not says the General & vanishes slowly
beginning with the broad
brim of his hat.
The grin remains for some time
after the rest of him has gone.

Author's Notes and Acknowledgments

I wish to thank experts at the Library of Virginia, the Louisa County Historical Society, the Bull Run Regional Library, the Fairfax County Circuit Court Historic Records Center, and the Fairfax County Public Library for their assistance in locating the archival documents which inform some of these poems.

My research was supported by the English Department at the University of Louisville, the University of Louisville's Commonwealth Center for the Humanities and Society, and the Virginia Foundation for the Humanities at the University of Virginia.

The poems of section 2 are inspired by two works of history: Andrew Levy's *The First Emancipator: Slavery, Religion, and the Quiet Revolution of Robert Carter* and John Randolph Barden's unpublished dissertation, "'Flushed with Notions of Freedom': The Growth and Emancipation of a Virginia Slave Community, 1732–1812" from Duke University.

The three untitled poems appearing at the beginning, midpoint, and end of this chapbook are inspired by Lewis Carroll's *Alice's Adventures in Wonderland*. They have been transformed into comics by poet and visual artist

Lauren Haldeman.

I'm grateful to Julia Kudravetz for her continuing friendship and for her hospitality during my time in Charlottesville.

My mother, Patricia Petrosino, accompanied me on two long road trips to Virginia so that I could pursue my research. We had many adventures together, and are planning more. This little book is for her, with love.

About the Author

Kiki Petrosino is the author of three books of poetry: *Hymn for the Black Terrific* (2013), *Fort Red Border* (2009), and *Witch Wife (2017)*, all from Sarabande Books. She holds graduate degrees from the University of Chicago and the University of Iowa Writer's Workshop. Her poems have appeared in Poetry, *Best American Poetry*, *The New York Times*, *FENCE*, *Gulf Coast*, *jubilat*, *Tin House*, and elsewhere. She is founder and co-editor of *Transom*, an independent online poetry journal. She is an Associate Professor of English at the University of Louisville, where she directs the Creative Writing Program.

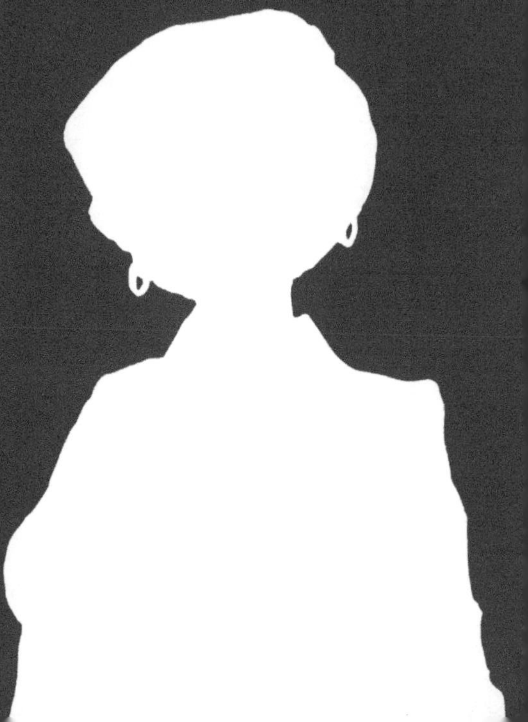

CPSIA information can be obtained
at www.ICGtesting.com
Printed in the USA
LVHW070406281119
638727LV00034B/4113/P

9 781942 083733